10.95

Be Fruitful and Multiply

J. W. Matlock, Sr., Ph.D.

VANTAGE PRESS
New York

Published by Vantage Press, Inc.
516 West 34th Street, New York, New York 10001

Manufactured in the United States of America
ISBN: 0-533-10920-5

Library of Congress Catalog Card No.: 93-95013

0 9 8 7 6 5 4 3 2 1

To my wife of thirty-one years, Glenda Faye Matlock

Contents

In Appreciation		vii
Introduction		ix
1.	For the Wrong Reason	1
2.	Why Do We Need a Church?	4
3.	Shame of the Barren Church	7
4.	The Barren Church and Prayer	12
5.	Time to Move Forward	16
6.	They Multiplied and Grew	22
7.	They Cried unto the Lord	30
Notes		33
Recommended Reading		35

In Appreciation

I wish to acknowledge the persons who so willingly assisted me in typing and proofreading the material that makes up *Be Fruitful and Multiply:* Kimberly Kelly and members of Central Full Gospel Fellowship.

To my wife, whose life has been dedicated to the work of the Lord for the past twenty years, for her patience and understanding through the many days of isolation, for the period of time during which I have been dedicated to the task of compiling this dissertation.

Introduction

Concerning this house which thou art in building, if thou wilt walk in my statutes, and execute my judgements, and keep all my commandments to walk in them, then I will perform my word with thee, which I spake unto David thy father. And I will dwell among the children of Israel, and will not forsake my people Israel.

—1 Kings 6:12–13

The church building is a building consecrated for divine worship of God. The church is also the body of Christ, Christ being the head.

There are more than a few questions about why we need a church building, why we spend so much money on buildings, why we need to go to a building to worship God, and why we want our membership to increase.

This dissertation is written for professional theologians and the many men and women who are not, in the hope of helping them find the answer.

I have made a conscious effort to keep the language simple and the explanations uncomplicated. Though a pastor myself, I have laypeople in view, primarily because they are the vast majority of God's people.

I kept the footnotes to a minimum and used them when necessary to document a statement or to make clear the subject of discussion and for proof of research.

The author, in his humble way and in the fear of God, has given prayer, meditation, and study in this dissertation titled *Be Fruitful and Multiply.*

Be Fruitful and Multiply

CHAPTER 1

For the Wrong Reason

I believe that today we have many churches that are conceived out of the will of God. Some organizations want as many church locations as the other organization down the street; or, if that man can build a church, then I can, too. A church that has been conceived through this kind of reasoning may grow in number but never in the Spirit of the Lord unless their reasoning and heart are changed.

Wagner reports that John Wimber researched churches of over two hundred members growing at 100 percent per decade or more. His findings: First, the pastors knew God had called them to the ministry. Second, he found that they knew they were called to their place of ministry.[1]

In Matthew 16:13–19, when Jesus came into the coasts of Caesarez Philippi, he questioned his disciples:

"Whom do men say that I the Son of man am?" And they said, "Some say that thou art John the Baptist, some Elijah, and others Jeremiah or one of the prophets." He said unto them, "But whom say ye that I am?" And Simon Peter answered and said, "Thou art the Christ, the Son of the living God." And Jesus answered and said unto him, "Blessed art thou, Simon Barjona, for flesh and blood hath not revealed it unto thee, but my Father which is in heaven. And I say unto thee that thou art Peter, and upon this rock

1

I will build my church; and the gates of hell shall not prevail against it. And I will give unto thee the keys of the kingdom of heaven and whatsoever thou shalt bind on earth shall be bound in heaven and whatsoever thou shalt loose on earth shall be loosed in heaven."

If the reason is not that the Lord has ordained this church, then it is for the wrong reason. However, as we can see from the above verses, Matthew 16:13–19, if God has ordained a particular work, it will succeed, that is, if it is built in complete obedience to God's will and at His pace, which is what we find most difficult, a church can succeed.

I will give you another example from 2 Samuel 7:1 that a church must be ordained of God, and when it is, God will provide all that is needed.

And it came to pass, when the king sat in his house, and the Lord had given him rest round about from all his enemies; that the king said unto Nathan the prophet, "See now, I dwell in a house of cedar, but the ark of God dwelleth within curtains." And Nathan said to the king, "Go, do all that is in thine heart; for the Lord is with thee." And it came to pass that night that the word of the Lord came unto Nathan saying, "Go tell my servant David, thus says the Lord, shalt thou build a house for me to dwell in? And when thy days be fulfilled, and thou shalt sleep with thy father, I will set up thy seed after thee, which shall proceed out of thy bowels, and will establish his kingdom. He shall build a house for my name, and I will establish the throne of his kingdom forever.

And in 1 Chronicles 22:6–10:

Then he called Solomon his son, and charged him to build a house for the Lord God of Israel. And David said unto

2

Solomon, "My son, as for me it was in my mind to build a house unto the name of the Lord my God: But the word of the Lord came to me saying, thou hast shed blood abundantly, and hast made great wars: thou shalt not build a house unto my name, because thou hast shed much blood upon the earth in my sight. Behold, a son shall be born to thee who shall be a man of rest; and I will give him rest from all his enemies round about, for his name shall be Solomon, and I will give peace and quietness unto Israel in his days. He shall build a house for my name; and he shall be my son, and I will be his father; and I will establish the throne of his kingdom over Israel forever.

A desire to build a church does not mean one has been ordained by God to do so. God must choose the person, place, and time; then and only then is it ordained of God.

I would like also to refer to James 4:13–17 as further reason for my view of the wrong reason for many churches being established:

Go to now, ye that say, today or tomorrow we will go into such a city, and continue there year, and buy and sell, and get gain: Whereas ye know not what shall be on the morrow. For what is your life? Is it even a vapor, that appeareth for a little time and then vanisheth away. For that ye ought to say, if the Lord will, we shall live, and do this or that. But now ye rejoice in your boasting; all such rejoicing is evil. Therefore to him that knoweth to do good, and doeth it not, to him it is sin.

As Gamaliel states in Acts 5:33–42, I can say, "Take heed to yourselves what you intend to do as touching this matter. . . . " If it is not of God, it will be scattered, and brought to nought. But if it be of God, you cannot overthrow it, lest haply you be found even to fight against God.

CHAPTER 2
Why Do We Need a Church?

When we look at the church, we view it through a traditional paradigm. We know churches have sanctuaries, pulpits, pews, and a clergy. For us it is difficult to think of a church without any of these familiar components. Critics of the church have been known to say that many of God's people started without any of the conveniences of today's church and did very well. I can only say to the critics that a great many of man's early efforts may have started without the luxuries we have today. These advances have enabled us to be more effective in our efforts to improve ourselves in such areas as health, education, etc. Therefore, their thinking does not have adequate support; if critics choose to judge the progress of the church, they should also judge the progress of the entire world.[1]

The question, "Why do we need a church?" can be answered when we ask, "Why are we here?" We are the salt of the earth. We are the light of the world. We must let our light shine before men that they may see our good works and glorify our Father which is in heaven. For this we need a place to be refreshed, taught, and to exhort one another.

And they, continuing daily with one accord in the temple, and breaking bread from house to house, did eat their meat with gladness and singleness of heart, praising God, and having favor with all the people. And the Lord added to the church daily such as should be saved.

—Acts 2:46–47

Or, as is said in 1 Corinthians 12:27:

Now we are the body of Christ, and member in particular.

We are the church, but why would one think that having a building is wrong or unnecessary? The church is a type of sheepfold for the many individual flocks. However, someone always seems to point out the fact that the church building is used only three or four times weekly. This is very true in most cases, but why have we not heard these same people speak out about our schools sitting vacant three months out of each year? Why do we not simply teach our children under a tree? Or one could raise the question of our lake houses that are only used once a year or the mobile trailer that has not been moved in two years. I believe anyone can see that believers need a regular meeting place.

As it says in I Peter 5:2:

Feed the flock of God which is among you, taking the oversight thereof, not by constraint but willingly; not for filthy lucre, but of a ready mind.

We need a regular meeting place because the word of God tells the believers to forsake not the assembling of ourselves.

Let us hold fast the profession of our faith without wavering, for He is faithful that promised. And let us consider one

5

another to provoke unto love and good works: not forsaking the assembling of ourselves together as the manner of some is; but exhorting one another, and so much the more, as ye see the day approaching.

—Hebrews 10:23–25

That thine eyes may be open upon this house day and night, upon this place whereof thou hast said that thou wouldest put thy name there; to hearken unto to the prayers which thy servant prayeth toward this place.

—2 Chronicles 6:20

For now have I chosen and sanctified this house, that my name may be there forever, and mine eyes and mine heart shall be there perpetually.

—2 Chronicles 7:16

If one has made up one's mind that believers do not need a place of worship, then there is nothing that I or anyone else could say to change that opinion. However, I will say this much on the subject; if one will go to church regularly for a few months, one then will begin to realize the importance of having a church building.

CHAPTER 3

Shame of the Barren Church

If thou wilt indeed look on the affliction of thine handmaid, and remember me, and not forget thine handmaid, but wilt give unto thine handmaid a man child, then I will give him unto thee, Lord . . . , Go in peace, and the God of Israel grant thee thy petition that thou hast asked of Him. . . .

If one will only take the time to read these Scriptures, they will be found refreshing to the church or Christian who is surprised or oppressed, unfruitful, and has been in a dormant state.

As one looks at Hannah as a type of a barren church, and sees how that God healed her barren womb, and that through God the church, which has set barren for years, may also become fruitful.

As it says in St. John 15:7–8:

If you abide in me, and my words abide in you, ye shall ask what ye will, and it shall be done unto you. Herein is my Father glorified, that ye bear much fruit, so shall ye be my disciples.

This Scripture is a truth directly from Christ. So if His word is in us, and we are living in His word, we should be fruitful. Let us dare to believe that as God healed Hannah and made her fruitful, so can He heal and make the barren church fruitful, a church that is growing.

Hannah was sorrowful because she was barren, unable to give her husband a son. Most will tell you as Christians we should be happy, and I agree. However, the word of God tells us there is a time for all things. I believe that when a church is barren, it is time to be sorrowful. What are we existing for if not to bring new life into existence?

Hannah believed that a child (life) was a gift of God, an inheritance from God. So Hannah was sorrowful because she had been deprived of this inheritance that God had given to other women.

We must ask ourselves, how sorrowful do we become when souls are not born into the kingdom of God because of the existence of this church? Also, how long has it been since you have heard men and women in the altars crying out to God, saying, "Lord, I just cannot go on not seeing souls being born into the kingdom because of this ministry. Lord, I can have no joy until this church becomes fruitful again." I can tell you, it has been too long. In most churches, prayer has become something to which we pay lip service. We say we believe in prayer, but we rarely get beyond a recitation of our prayers or a barrage of requests that we want God to answer at His earliest convenience.

Men have been too busy praying for themselves for long life, prosperity, and joy. How long has it been since you have seen the church sorely vexed and moved into an old-fashioned revival because the church was barren?

I believe the church should be impressed with Hannah because she was sorrowful due to her inability to give to her husband, her lord, a son. Hannah's adversary provoked her sore and made her fret because the Lord had shut up her womb because she had given no son to her husband.

Now I ask you, how long, how long will it be until the

churches of God come to the place where we are humili-
ated, where we are ashamed because the worldly churches
are growing and point their finger and mock because we
are barren? Our buildings are in decay and our parking lots
are overgrown because there is no life being produced.

There are some 375,000 churches in the United States,
and most of them are small. In the Leith Anderson Report,
it shows that half of these churches have seventy-five or
fewer at worship on a typical Sunday morning, while most
are stable. However, many are built upon and held together
by permanent family relationships and not a sorrow for lost
souls, or they expect the lost to come to them.[1]

Hannah was sorrowful because her womb was barren.
Yet many churches are without any shame or sorrow in
spite of the fact that there has not been one soul saved
because of their existence.

Hannah might have said, "I have been a wife; it is not
my fault that I have no child." I think that possibly this is
the attitude of many of the churches today. We have tried.
We have been here for years. We have used all of our
energy—trying to get the lost to come to us. It is not our
fault we have not grown.

But maybe it is. What is the role of the church in the
world? What is the work before us, and who is responsible
to do the work?

Go ye therefore, and teach all nations, baptizing them in the
name of the Father, and of the Son, and of the Holy Ghost,
teaching them to observe all things whatsoever I have
commanded you, and lo, I am with you always, even unto
the end of the world.
—Matthew 28:19–20

Ye are the light of the world. A city that is set on a hill cannot

9

be hid. Neither do men light a candle, and put it under a bushel but on a candlestick; and it giveth light unto all that are in the house. Let your light so shine before men, that they may see your good works, and glorify your Father which is in heaven.

—Matthew 5:14–16

As thou hast sent me into the world, even so have I also sent them into the world.

—St. John 17:18

Hannah's husband had sons and daughters, but this did not matter to her. She was not personally involved in giving one of them to her husband, and this gave her much sorrow and so she wept before the Lord. I do not believe there is any hope for a church until they become so sorrowful that they have become or been so barren and unfruitful in soul-winning until they cannot eat or drink until God allows them to become fruitful.

The church is the body of Christ:

And He is the head of the body, the church; who is the beginning, the firstborn from the dead; that in all things He might have the pre-eminence.

—Colossians 1:18

The body of Christ is what produces life. And although each local church makes up that body, we each still have a responsibility to produce life (new life) for God. There is nothing wrong on God's end to bring new life into being. That is, the price forever is paid. So if the church is not giving birth, then there is something wrong with that body, with that particular womb.

10

Praising God, and having favor with all people. And the Lord added to the church daily such as should be saved.

—Acts 2:47

Do you know what this church had been doing? They had been in much prayer, and daily they continued with one accord. When a church becomes barren, it is because its members have become barren. Members become barren because they have seen their own saved and have forgotten the great commission: "Go ye into all the world, and preach the gospel to every creature."

The fact that Hannah's barren womb was made fruitful because she was sorrowful, and knowing that there is ready help for all that will be fruitful, we should be refreshed.

If ye abide in me, and my words abide in you, ye shall ask what ye will, and it shall be done unto you. Herein is my Father glorified, that ye bear much fruit, so shall ye be my disciples.

—St. John 15:7–8

However, knowing that God is able to make, and is glorified in the church and in each individual being made fruitful, there is a danger in being unfruitful and content.

Every branch in me that beareth not fruit he taketh away.

—St. John 15:2

11

CHAPTER 4

The Barren Church and Prayer

Hannah prayed unto the Lord, and wept sore because she
was barren.

—1 Samuel 1:10

Her body was not able to do what God had created it to do.
Notice that Hannah did not blame God nor her husband.
She did not attack those who mocked her, and most of all,
she did not make excuses for her barrenness. But what she
did do was pray unto God.

The beautiful thing is that she let her pain, her unfruitful condition, drive her to prayer, and that place of prayer
became a place of blessing for her. In every church we hear
people complain about lost members in their families, but
how often do we see it drive them to a place of prayer?

Some years ago Central Full Gospel, the church that I
pastor, had stopped growing. We were very active in visi-
tation work, and visitors were passing through each service; but we had no growth. No souls were being saved, and
most were complaining about the lack of growth. Not knowing what else to do, I laid before God for guidance. God
showed me what it would take for Central to grow. God told
me to have a week of prayer, a prayer revival. So for a week,
we came together each night and would have a few congre-
gational songs, a testimony or two, and it would be a

12

service just about like any other service except for the preaching of the word. Where we usually had forty-five minutes to an hour of preaching, we had the congregation praying. Within two months Central Full Gospel had doubled, and we were building a new auditorium. "We have not because we ask not."

However, Hannah's prayer included a vow: "If you will remember me, and not forget thine handmaid, but will give unto thine handmaid a child, then I will give him unto the Lord all the days of his life." Church, what are we praying for? We have become so sidetracked that we have forgotten what the purpose of the church is.

But seek ye first the kingdom of God, and his righteousness and all these things shall be added unto you.
—Matthew 6:33

That is, if the church (the believers) will get back to soul winning and stop fretting over what we are going to eat or drink, God will add all these things and the church will once again begin to be added to.

Do we want people or souls? When we pray, is it for the wrong reason? Do we just want a bigger number than the church across town? Could it be that we are not concerned with giving God a son, but only having one more in our number to boast about?

We pray, we vow, God allows us to grow. Lord, we will feed and care for all you give us. But all too often when God gives growth, we forget our mission and our vows. We become too involved with entertaining the numbers so we will not lose them, that we have no time to care for their souls. God will not send people where they will not be fed and cared for.

13

He said unto him the third time . . . , feed my sheep.

—St. John 21:17

George Barna points out that when a challenge arises, the church attempts to design a system that will handle the situation effectively. We refer to these systems as our programs. There is only one problem with this strategy: ministry. Ministry, or feeding God's sheep, is not about programs. Ministry is about people. The Scripture tells us by words and deeds our focus is to be on people through meaningful relationships. Ministry means getting involved in the life of people who need support.[1]

Go in peace, and the God of Israel grant thee thy petition that thou has asked of him. So the woman went . . . , and her countenance was no more sad. Hannah had joy because she would have a man child. God can heal the barren church as well. A church need not be unfruitful or dormant; one should forget about the bad location or the fact that most of the church membership is over fifty-five and know that God can make the barren womb fruitful and give a new countenance. Joy will never come to a life or church that is unfruitful.

The new countenance comes with a testimony. Hannah had a testimony: "I am she that was barren, I am she that was so vexed in soul that I could not lift up my voice in the house of God. But now I have a son that I asked from God." The church will have a testimony when we can bring forth a son that God has given us because we ask of God. When we have a testimony, we shall also have a new countenance.

Hannah's blessing came only because she would not be content in and with an unfruitful life. Only when the church will refuse to be content in a dormant state will we

14

begin to pray, and the fervent prayer of a righteous man availeth much.

Confess your faults one to another, and pray one for another, that ye may be healed. The effectual fervent prayer of a righteous man availeth much.

—James 5:16

CHAPTER 5

Time to Move Forward

In Deuteronomy 2:1–7, God spoke to Israel and said, "Ye have compassed this mountain long enough; turn you northward."

I would like to draw from these Scriptures to make a statement: the church must keep moving forward. The church must keep growing.

As Christians we are blessed in many ways. However, because of these blessings, we are often in danger of being hindered where the work of God is concerned.

Many times when a church such as Central Full Gospel has been blessed by God and has grown to a comfortable size, it is easy to sit back and get too comfortable and satisfied. That is dangerous because we must continue to move forward. There is yet another danger. In being blessed with so much that we get wrapped up in self-confidence, we move out before God gives us the go-ahead, which can be equally dangerous.

Let us liken this mountain to the place where the church gets comfortable or confident; a comfortable number may be fifty for some churches and five hundred for others.

This mountain was not a bad place, and there was nothing wrong with Israel compassing the mountain many days, but it was not where God wanted them to remain. It was a resting place. However, the trouble with a resting place is that it is very easy to get so comfortable that one simply cannot get started again.

I believe this is where many of the churches in America stand today. We have been blessed in every way. We have a nice building, an average-sized congregation, and enough financial support to take care of all the expenses, so this must be where God wants us to stay. Not so. As long as there is one lost soul, the church has not grown to the size God wants us to be. God is saying to all, it is time to move, grow, not time to get comfortable.

> Say, know ye, there are yet four months, and then cometh harvest? Behold, I say unto you, lift up your eyes, and look on the fields; for they are white already to harvest. And they that reapeth receiveth wages, and gathereth fruit unto life eternal; that both he that soweth and he that reapeth may rejoice together.
>
> —St. John 4:35–36

I ask you, do we believe the church has accomplished all that God has ordained it to? If your answer is no, and I believe that it is, then we cannot be satisfied with where we are as a person or a church now, or tomorrow.

The place where one was in their Christian walk a year ago was all right a year ago, but not today. The place where the church was at that time last year was sufficient for last year. However, it is not sufficient for today. I believe that when a church stays in one place, without spiritual or numerical growth, they are in danger of spiritual incest taking place. I am not saying all churches must grow to over a hundred members; there will always be small churches because of their geographical location. Where there is no growth, there is no new life, no new ideals, and often no vision.

In all thy ways acknowledge him, and he shall direct thy paths.
—Proverbs 3:6

Commit thy ways unto the Lord; trust also in him and he shall bring it to pass.
—Psalm 37:5

By committing ourselves unto God, we find first what He wants us to be as a church, then what He wants us to do; see that they are cared for. To quote George Barna:

An organization is most successful not when it seeks to become the biggest or the broadest, but when it strives to be the best in its own focused area of expertise. [Barna goes on to say,] Sadly, most churches have yet to understand the application of this principle to their ministry. Simply put, a church cannot be all things to all people. However, we must be an all-people church. The stark reality is that every church has limited resources, and has been called to accomplish a specific mission. Despite the urge to be all things to all people, the successful churches resisted that impulse to be the answer to everyone's individual problems by focusing in their vision for ministry, by reaffirming their commitment to quality, and recognizing their limitations.[1]

If we go back to Deuteronomy 2:3, God said to Israel, "Ye have compassed this mountain long enough, turn you northward." This is the way that God wanted Israel to move; this was the only way to the land that God had promised them.

Lift up your eyes, and look on the fields, for they are white already to harvest.

—St. John 4:35

The church must see that God is calling us to move forward; the direction to move is toward the lost, the fields that are white to harvest. We are running out of time. We cannot be satisfied with where we are or with what we are doing.

When ye shall have done all those things which are commanded you, say, "We are unprofitable servants, we have done that which was our duty to do."

—Luke 17:10

Have we done all He has commanded us to do? Not until we have left no stone unturned.

One of the problems the church has with moving forward is the same problem men have with turning to God for salvation. They are afraid they will have to give something up. The church wants to take the mountain with her. The Lord said if you believe, you can say unto this mountain, "Be thou moved"; so we are not going to move until it does. But this mountain is not for us, it is for those following us. We can have faith in God for our journey. He will direct each step. Has it not been God, all God, which has brought us to this place? Then it is also God whom we can trust to help us reach the next step in our growth.

The Lord said to Israel, "I have blessed thee in all the works of thy hand." He knoweth thy walking through this great wilderness these forty years thy God hath been with thee; thou hast lacked nothing.

—Deuteronomy 2:7

19

In August 1978, I was working in an Assembly of God Church in Forth Worth, Texas. I and my family were very happy there, and I had thought nothing about moving because souls were being saved through my ministry. I had found my mountain. Then came the call that would change my life forever: you have compassed this mountain long enough. At this point I believed God would have me start a new work, but where, and why me? I knew this much: I surely could not do it unless God opened every door.

Go to now, ye that say, today or tomorrow we will . . . and get gain. Whereas ye know not what shall be on tomorrow.

—James 4:13, 15

I truly believed if I acknowledged the Lord, He would direct my path. In fact, the Lord told me if I would obey and follow him, he would supply all that was needed. For lack of space, I will just say here, in fifteen years, Central Full Gospel has grown from thirteen members to one hundred seventy-five active members. God has also given us a new auditorium that will seat four hundred people and full renovation of the existing building, all of which is paid for. Why? Because God called, I answered, answered the call to seek the lost.

Central grows because we know there is no time to get satisfied as long as there is one lost soul in our city, and there are many. You see God has promised in his word:

My God shall supply all my needs according to His riches in glory by Christ Jesus.

—Philippians 4:19

I know that in many cases it is hard for a church to think about moving forward when it is all they can do just

to stay alive. However, let me assure you that God will take care of you as you make up your mind and do not sit still to die.

Second Kings 6–7 tells how in Samaria, many churches had made themselves secure behind their walls. The only thing wrong with their plan was that their safety became their curse. Syria gathered all of its hosts, went up, and besieged Samaria. And to make matters worse, there was a famine in the land, much like the spiritual famine in many of the churches today. So Syria besieged it until the people of Samaria began to starve; they began to eat their own children.

When a church tries to secure itself behind its walls, it can be sure that it is only a matter of time until the power of darkness will besiege it until the members devour themselves. Good advice came from the four leprous men at the city's gate. They did what the church must do. We should ask ourselves, "Why sit we here until we die?" If we enter into the city, the famine is in the city (a church that will not move forward), and we shall die there. If we sit still here, we die also. Let us move forward. If they save us alive, we shall live, and if they kill us, we shall but die.

When only a few in the church make up their minds that they will not sit still and die or let the church die, they can be sure that God will save them and the church alive, that we shall live.

CHAPTER 6
They Multiplied and Grew

But the more they afflicted them, the more they multiplied
and grew.

—Exodus 1:12

I would like for you to view the new king over Egypt, which
knew not Joseph (Exodus 1:8), as a type of darkness or evil
that is in the world today that has afflicted the church
unless we multiply, keep up the fight against it, and get out
of the land.

One of the first things any church must understand is
that opposition or affliction is not a signal to stop and
retreat. The church cannot stop moving forward, working
for growth just because we are being afflicted or because
we have become tired and have not grown as fast as we had
envisioned. However, it is my opinion that this is actually
what is occurring.

It has been expressed to me by more than a few that
our church has not grown because no one wants to hear
the truth, that our standards are too high for others to
follow, for God said there would be a great falling away in
the last days. Knowing that God has ordained the church
to bring forth much fruit, statements such as these can only
be viewed as excuses.

I am not saying that numbers mean success, and I fully

agree with George Barna, who points out that the Scriptures suggest that a church is a blessing if it is changing people's lives by bringing them into a deeper relationship with God, through faith in Christ and the indwelling power of the Holy Spirit. The church that blesses people in this way is a church that will grow spiritually and numerically. Barna also points out that the 300,000 plus congregations in America are increasing the number of people who attend their worship services by at least 10 percent each year. However, there are many churches across the nation that are growing because they believe the Great Commission in Matthew 28:19–20.[1]

These are churches that will not justify no growth just because they have reached a comfortable number, knowing that there are still lost souls to reach; and its members will come into contact with many of them each day. This, I believe, gives most churches the ability to grow.

C. Peter Wagner said:

First, the pastor must want the church to grow and be willing to pay the price. Second, the people must want the church to grow and be willing to pay the price. Five special prices that a pastor must pay for church growth are assuming the responsibility for growth, working hard, sharing the ministry, having members he cannot pastor (one-on-one relationships), and revising the no-growth theology. For the members they are agreeing to follow growth leadership, paying the money, readjusting their fellowship groups, and opening their leadership circles.[2]

The church today, just as Israel did in Egypt, finds itself without friends. God led them into Egypt under Joseph's care, but Joseph was dead, and so were all those who had made life in Egypt easy for them. Now they were alone and friendless. That actually was not the case at all.

In chapter 1, I stated that the church at large started with nothing; no buildings, no pews, none of the things we enjoy today. We must know without any doubt that God calls and places us where we are, just as He did Israel in Egypt. If this fact has been settled, and it must be, then we can be sure that we are not without a friend. In fact, we have the greatest friend of all: God Himself. Matthew 28:20 reads: "Lo, I am with you always." What I am saying is that not unlike Israel after the death of Joseph, the leaders did not have the faith or vision that Joseph had when he found himself sold into Egypt and God his only friend. Regardless of our numbers, when the church loses its faith and vision, it has become no more than a social group. I believe the church is under much affliction, yet just as Israel, the more we are afflicted the more we must grow and multiply.

Matthew 9:38 reads: "The harvest fields are white . . ."

1 Corinthians 3:6 reads: "I have planted, Apollos watered, but God gave the increase."

2 Peter 3:9 reads: " . . . not willing that any should perish, but that all should come to repentance."

Luke 15:7 reads: "There is joy in heaven over one sinner who repents."

In short, it is God's will that churches grow, and someone in heaven must be keeping close count. The fact that the church is being afflicted is no excuse not to grow or see souls saved. Therefore, I ask you, why have so many for so long used it for an excuse?

This church, all believers, have descended from Christ and have become this great multitude. However, much like Israel, their multitude does not have the confidence in God that Christ or Joseph had within themselves. Thus, we

deem ourselves friendless and sometimes hopeless because Christ has been received up into heaven.

Have we forgotten that Christ said He would not leave
us without a friend?

> I will pray the Father, and he shall give you another com-
> forter, that he may abide with you forever.
>
> —St. John 14:16

> It is expedient for you that I go away, for if I go not away, the
> comforter will not come unto you. But if I depart, I will send
> him unto you.
>
> —St. John 16:7

We can be greatly encouraged by this knowledge because unlike the Comforter, God sent Israel, namely Moses.
He will not run out when the going gets hard. Yet the church
has cried out, "My God, why have you forsaken us?" He has
not. The arm of flesh that the church has turned to trust in
the system, has failed them.

Growth means change, and any change brings pain.
The church is not unlike Israel's state as they prayed for
deliverance from Egypt. In order for them to have a better
life, they had to be freed from Pharaoh's oppression. However, when God made evident the way and the man He had
chosen for the job, Israel began to complain.

> And they said unto them, "The Lord look upon you and
> judge; because ye have made our savor to be abhorred in
> the eyes of his servants . . . "
>
> —Exodus 5:21

Why? The answer is the same as always. The change
brought more hard work; the hard work brought pain.

The church knows we must grow if we are to do the

will of God, and God's plan is clear in His word. And yet so often as the pastor, the man whom God has chosen for the job, tries to promote growth, the congregation can only complain because they are asked to work harder.

The theme is still the same. Matthew 28:19 reads: "Go ye therefore, and teach all nations . . . ," and Christ said in Acts 1:8: "After the Holy Ghost has come upon you, and you shall be witnesses unto me . . . unto the uttermost part of the earth."

It is all for one end; that souls may be saved, and when this is occurring, the church is growing. Allow me to state this in another way: the church is friendless in the world today. For the most part, the world's system is against the church.

> If the world hates you, ye know that it hated me before it hated you. If ye were of the world, the world would love his own; but because I have chosen you out of the world, therefore the world hateth you.
>
> —St. John 15:18–19

> Ye have not chosen me, but I have chosen you, and ordained you that ye should bring forth fruit, and that your fruit should remain.
>
> —St. John 15:16

Any way one tries to say it, it still comes out the same. The church must grow if it is obeying the Great Commission.

Israel had been laboring under very cruel conditions, but now the straw was taken away. We can see how they might be discouraged; their effort was in vain.

As many of the churches in America steadily decline or fight just to keep the few they have, to talk of growth is to ask them to make brick without straw. Under such conditions it is no wonder the people are complaining. However, we must ask ourselves this question: have we been laboring for the wrong reason?

Israel's labor was for Pharaoh, to build him large cities, not houses for themselves, nor for God's glory. Has the labor of the church been only to deliver a number for some man or organization with little or no concern for the lost souls? Has it been that the church has become too dependent upon the system, the Pharaoh straw, to build the church? Can it be that our trust in programs more than the Spirit of God has sent a message to the world that we are no different from them?

When a church takes a real stand for Christ, the world can see the difference in us. We trust in God, not the Pharaoh straw. Ours is a labor of love, not the labor of those in bondage. Yes, the labor of the church is abhorred in the eyes of the world; nevertheless, we may rejoice because we know that as we labor we are freeing men from Satan's cruel bondage and keeping the Great Commission. The church does not need the system; the system is of the world, and it most certainly has not done much for the world, except encourage it to try to devour one another.

Israel, as a church, labored with intense effort under the Egyptian system. Theirs was not a labor of love, nor even a meaningful labor, only a forced labor under a master who hated them. This should make each of us see just how cruel the master of this world is, just how cruel the god of this world can be and how he oppresses his servants.

This is an example of the condition under which the church must labor among the world and the wickedness. However, all the men and women who are unsaved can be seen in a type of bondage placed upon them by the god of this world without hope of anything better unless the church leaves the comfort of its four walls and goes into Egypt to deliver them from their bondage.

I am not saying that it will be easy. We have our work cut out for us trying to reach men and women under the control of Satan. We know that he will not let them go without a fight, but the church cannot give up just because Satan has such a hold on them. They are in bondage. They are serving the Devil, and he is making their lives grievous; he hates them, and they think he loves them, but we know differently.

So the work of the church must intensify because we see the closing hours of this age of grace and know the sad bondage the world is under; we know the affliction that will come upon us as we labor. The church has suffered under adverse circumstances. We have labored and toiled just to keep what we have, the same tale of bricks. The church has not had time to evangelize; we have spent all of our time and resources trying to keep the few members we have.

I cannot tell you how many times I have had church leaders say to me, "I am concerned about growth, but more concerned about keeping the members we have." We do not have time to seek the lost; it takes all our time trying to keep members faithful in church.

We had a hundred this Sunday morning; twenty-five of them were visitors. If we could only get our own to show up, we would be growing. All the leaders know the church must grow if we are to fulfill the Great Commission. Allow me to give you another example:

A certain nobleman went into a far country to receive for himself a kingdom, and to return. And he called his ten servants and delivered them ten pounds and said unto them, occupy until I come . . . When the nobleman returned, he rewarded and punished according to their faith-fulness.

—St. Luke 19:11–27

The members of the church are the pounds; that is, each must use his or her talent to help build the church that is seeing the lost receive salvation.

Let me give you another Scripture:

Not forsaking the assembling of ourselves together, as in the manner of some is; but exhorting one another, and so much the more as ye see the day approaching.

—Hebrews 10:25

What can we do? The church is going to awaken and realize that we must all be independent while remaining dependent upon one another. We must make sure that we are part of the solution and not part of the problem. We must make sure we are the ones who come out to visit, and not the ones who must be visited each week so we will be in church on Sunday.

As it says in Matthew 28:19–20:

Each of us have a commission; go ye therefore and teach all nations.

CHAPTER 7
They Cried unto the Lord

Now therefore, behold, the cry of the children of Israel is come unto me, and I have also seen the oppression wherewith the Egyptian (world) oppress them (the church).
—Exodus 3:9

The prayer of Israel was earnest and God heard their cry.

The effectual fervent prayer of a righteous man availeth much.
—James 5:16

Israel was not crying unto the taskmasters, but unto God. And may I point out that it was the affliction that drove them to prayer. Although we have dealt with prayer in chapter four, I point this out again because all too often we wait until we have tried everything else and then we turn to prayer. Only when the church becomes sick of being afflicted by Satan's system and again calls upon God, when we pray, "God, your way is the only way, God, deliver us from this place of bondage: no lost souls being saved, no new faces, no growth. Lord heal these fruitless wombs, and let us bring forth new life," will the church begin to grow.

It is sad, but the altar in most churches is the last place that ever needs repair or replacing because it just does not have that much use. God knows He must give the increase, and God is faithful to all who call upon Him.

> And the Lord added to the church daily such as should be saved.
>
> —Acts 2:47

I am going to see my loved ones saved, and I am hoping to see yours saved, also. Christ came that the lost may be saved, and that means church growth. I am convinced that when the church turns away from the system and back to God, saying not our way, not what we want, but Your will, then we will see the church move into a place where we will not need to worry about church growth.

There will be affliction, and we need to know this beforehand. The more a person or church presses in for God, the more the pressure is going to come against them. However, the bright side is that we have the sweet comfort of the Holy Spirit, and with this, we have one another to walk with who know the affliction in this Christian walk.

As the church moves out to keep the Great Commission, it will have much affliction, but in our affliction, we can grow as believers and as a church. We must if we are going to keep His commission.

As long as there is one lost soul, God wants the church to grow by one more soul. You may not agree completely with this opinion; however, I believe as Christians we all believe we must win the lost for Christ; and this is growth.

> And God blessed them, and God said unto them, "Be fruitful and multiply and replenish the earth, and subdue it, and have dominion . . . "
>
> —Genesis 1:28

31

Notes

Chapter 1. For the Wrong Reason
1. Wagner, C. Peter, *Leading Your Church to Growth* (Ventura, CA: Regal Books, 1984), p. 43.

Chapter 2. Why Do We Need a Church?
1. Peterson, Jim, *Church without Walls* (Colorado Springs : Nave Press, 1992), p. 18.

Chapter 3. Shame of the Barren Church
1. *Church without Walls* (Colorado Springs: Nave Press, 1992), p. 113.

Chapter 4. The Barren Church and Prayer
1. Barna, George, *Marketing the Church* (Colorado Springs: Nave Press, 1988), pp. 42–43.

Chapter 5. Time to Move Forward
1. Barna, George, *User Friendly Church* (Ventura, CA: Regal Books, 1991), pp. 50–51.

Chapter 6. They Multiplied and Grew
1. *User Friendly Church* (Ventura, CA: Regal Books, 1991), pp. 15, 24.
2. *Leading Your Church to Growth* (Ventura, CA: Regal Books, 1984), pp. 44–70.

Recommended Reading

Barna, George. *Marketing the Church*. Colorado Springs: Nave Press, 1988.

———. *User Friendly Church*. Ventura, CA: Regal Books, 1991.

Crabb, Dr. William, and Jeff Jernigan. *The Church in Ruins*. Colorado Springs: Nave Press, 1991.

Dudley, Carl S. *Making the Small Church Effective*. Nashville: Parthenon Press, 1978.

Gorman, Marvin. *Call to Victory*. New Orleans: Marvin Gorman Ministries, 1982.

Henderson, Robert Thornton. *Beating the Churchgoing Blahs*. Downers Grove, IL: Robert Thornton Henderson, 1986.

Lindgren, Alvin J., and Norman Shawchuck. *Let My People Go*. Nashville: Abingdon Press, 1980.

Pannenberg, Wolfhant. *The Church*. Philadelphia: Westminster Press, 1977.

Peterson, Jim. *Church without Walls*. Colorado Springs: Naves Press, 1992.

Tillapaugh, Frank R. *Unleashing the Church*. Ventura, CA: Regal Books, 1982.

Towns, Elmer C. *Ten of Today's Most Innovative Churches*. Ventura, CA: Regal Books, 1990.

Wagner, C. Peter. *Leading Your Church to Growth*. Ventura, CA: Regal Books, 1984.

Zimmerman, Thomas F., ed. *And He Gave Pastors*. Springfield, MO: Gospel Publishing House, 1979.